Scholastic's

The Magic School Bus

Science Explorations

A

SCHOLASTIC INC.

Senior Vice President, Director of Education: Dr. Ernest Fleishman
Editor in Chief: Catherine Vanderhoof
Managing Editor: Sandy Kelley
Written by Richard Chevat
Science Consultant: Pauline Lang
Vice President, Director, Editorial Design and Production: Will Kefauver
Project Art Director: Joan Michael
Art Director: Kathy Massaro
Cover illustration and interior illustrations: John Speirs
Assistant Production Director: Bryan Samolinski

Based on the award-winning Magic School Bus books by Joanna Cole, illustrated by Bruce Degen.
Based on the Magic School Bus animated television series produced by Scholastic Productions Inc.

Copyright © 1994 by Scholastic Inc.
All rights reserved. Published by Scholastic Inc.
Printed in the U.S.A.
ISBN 0-590-48766-3
2 3 4 5 6 7 8 9 10 14 99 98 97 96 95

Table of Contents

Meet the Friz....................4

Outta Space
        The Solar System...............7
What's for Lunch?
        The Food Chain.................12
Rub a Dub
        Forces.........................16
Mix Masters
        Beginning Chemistry...........20
It's in the Air
        Weather.......................24
The Grass Is Greener
        Seeds.........................28

Ant Antics
        Ants..........................32
Home—Not Alone
        Habitats......................36
Zounds!
        Sound.........................40
Something to Chew On
        Digestion.....................46
What Rot!
        Decomposition.................50
Is It Catching?
        Germs.........................54
Dry Up!
        Deserts.......................58

Hi, I'm Arnold. Welcome to our class. This is not like other classes. Funny things happen here. That's because of our teacher, Ms. Frizzle . . .

We all like Ms. Frizzle. But things in her class can get strange. Like when we go on field trips.

Did you say something about a field trip, Arnold?

I like field trips. Going to the zoo is a field trip. The problem is, Ms. Frizzle thinks going to the moon is a field trip.

So get ready to go to some strange places. And when you go on a trip, use this book to write down everything that happens.

Have you ever gone on a **field trip**? Where did you go? Or where would you like to go? Write or draw your answer.

Outta Space

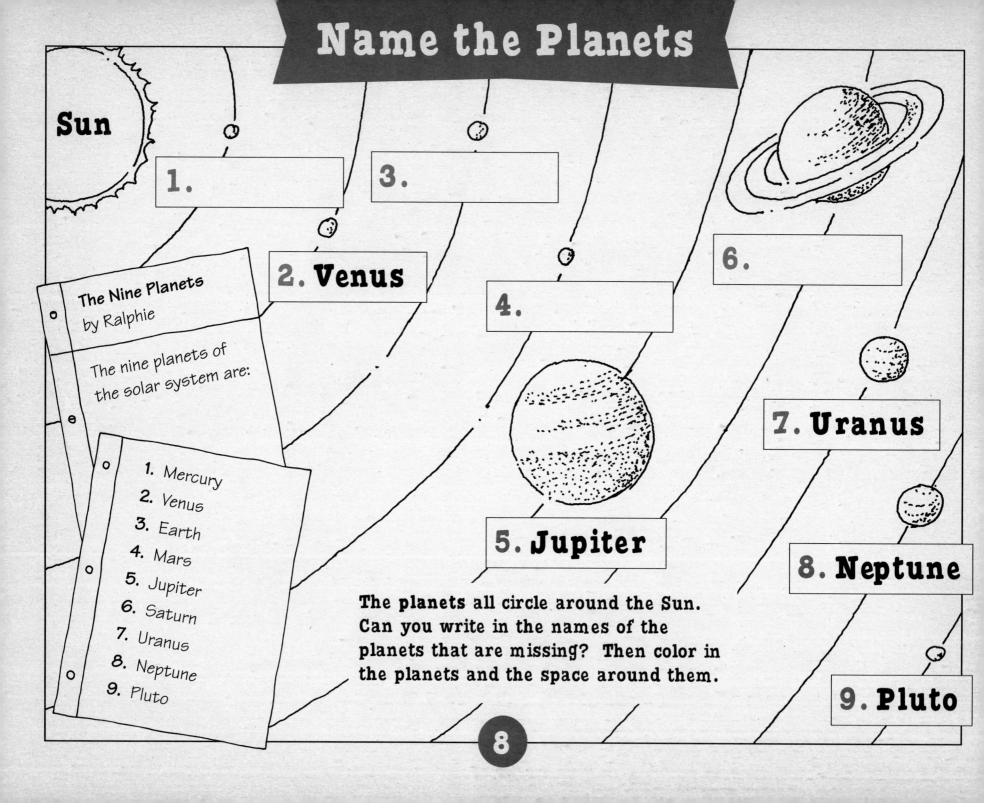

Name the Planets

Sun

1.

2. Venus

3.

4.

5. Jupiter

6.

7. Uranus

8. Neptune

9. Pluto

The Nine Planets
by Ralphie

The nine planets of the solar system are:

1. Mercury
2. Venus
3. Earth
4. Mars
5. Jupiter
6. Saturn
7. Uranus
8. Neptune
9. Pluto

The **planets** all circle around the Sun.
Can you write in the names of the
planets that are missing? Then color in
the planets and the space around them.

The Red Planet

Every planet is different. Look, there's Mars!

The only planet I want to see is good old Earth.

Mars, the Red Planet
by Tim

Mars is different from Earth. There is almost no water on Mars. The ground is red. It has two small moons. Things would weigh less on Mars than on Earth.

What do you think it would be like on Mars?
Read Tim's homework paper and draw a picture below.

Spinning Tops

As Earth circles around the Sun,
it also spins. As Earth spins,
we go from day to night and back.
You can see how this works.
You'll need a **ball** and a **flashlight**.
The flashlight is the Sun.
The ball is Earth.

Class, the planets and their moons all spin like tops.

My head is spinning from this trip.

1. Have a friend hold the flashlight.

2. Shine the light on the ball. Where the light falls on "Earth," it is day.

3. Put a small piece of tape on the ball.

4. Turn the ball slowly. Watch the tape move from light to dark.

In the square marked **DAY**, draw a picture of the ball when the tape is in the light. In the square marked **NIGHT**, draw a picture of the ball when the tape is in the dark.

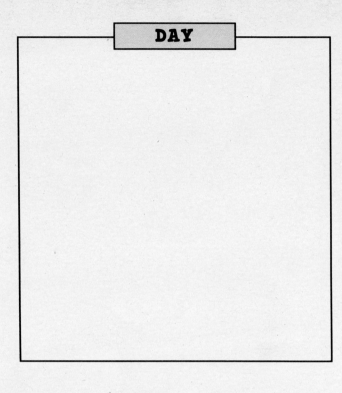

DAY

NIGHT

What if you were very small and could stand on the tape?
What would the flashlight look like to you?
Draw that below.

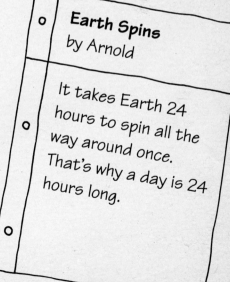

Earth Spins
by Arnold

It takes Earth 24 hours to spin all the way around once. That's why a day is 24 hours long.

What's for Lunch?

Ms. Frizzle says all living things need food—just like you. Some food comes from plants, and some comes from animals.

Now can we eat?

Eat! What a wonderful idea! Class, on the bus!

What Is Food?
by Ralphie

All living things need food for energy. Green plants make their own food. Animals eat plants or other animals.

Take a look in your lunch box.

What foods in your lunch came from plants? Write or draw them in one box. In the other box, write or draw the foods that came from animals.

PLANTS	ANIMALS

Who Eats What?

Look! That big fish is going to eat that little fish.

As long as it doesn't try to eat us.

Some animals eat plants. Some animals eat other animals. They are all part of a **food chain.** Look at the food chain below. Who eats what?

Food Chains
by Carlos

Almost every food chain begins with a plant. The sun helps plants make food. So almost every food chain starts with the sun.

| SEEDS | MOUSE | SNAKE | HAWK |

The mouse eats _____.

The snake eats _____.

The hawk eats _____.

In the box, draw or write one food that each animal eats.

I like being on a food chain—when it's time for lunch!

COW

PERSON

WOLF

BIG FISH

Rub a Dub

Things rubbing together cause a force called friction.

Some things have more friction than others. Try rubbing your hands together. Can you feel the friction? Now put some lotion on your hands and try again. Can you feel the difference? There is still friction, but not as much.

Why does a rolling marble stop?

Friction makes a rolling marble slow down and stop. What things cause more friction? Find out with a marble launcher.

piece of cardboard

1. Set up a marble launcher like the one in the picture. Put it on a bare floor.

2. Put a marble at the top of the launcher. Let go.

3. Use a ruler to measure from the marble launcher to where the marble stopped. In the chart, write down how far it went.

4. Try your launcher on a carpet, a large piece of cardboard, and on other kinds of floors. What caused the most friction?

_____

What caused the least? _____

MY FRICTION CHART	
Type of floor	**How far**

Moving Machines

Sometimes people use machines to make things move.

Our bus is a machine. It makes us move!

Pushing and Pulling
by Phoebe

Pushes and pulls are forces. They can make things move or make them stop. Friction is one kind of "pull."

Machines are tools that make it easier to push and pull.
A lever is a kind of a machine.

You can see how a lever works. You will need a very heavy book, a small block, and a wooden ruler.

1

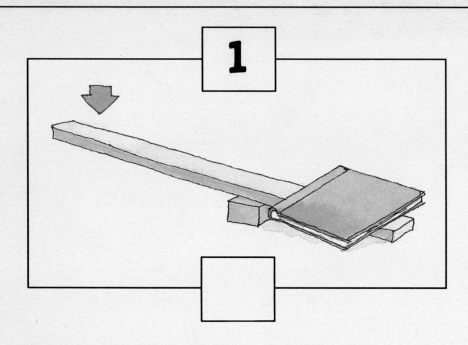

2

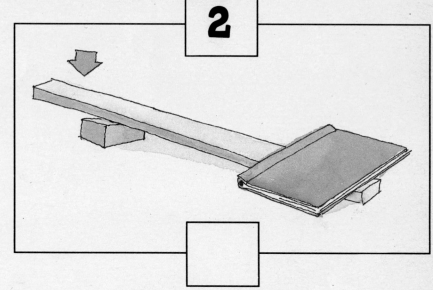

MY BEST LEVER

Look at the two pictures. Which way do you think will be easier to lift the book? Put a ✓ under that picture.

Try both ways.

Which lever was easier?   1   2

Was your guess right?_____

Try some other ways. Move the block. Use a bigger block. Use a longer lever. Draw the best lever you made.

Mix Masters

Take chances. Make mistakes. Get messy! That's the way to learn.

Then I must be learning a lot!

Every time you mix two things together, you're making a **mixture**.

1. Get a few foods you want to mix. On the next page, write or draw your list under FOODS BEFORE MIXING.

2. Look at each one. How does it taste? How does it feel? How does it smell? What does it look like?

3. Mix the foods together in a bowl. Taste your mixture. Can you taste the different parts?

4. Now, take the foods back out if you can. Look at each one. Has it changed? Write or draw what you found under FOODS AFTER MIXING.

Gobs of Goo

Sometimes, mixing two things together changes them.

Here is an easy recipe for making something strange.

You'll need:

$\frac{1}{2}$ **cup (125 ml) cornstarch**

$\frac{1}{2}$ **cup (125 ml) water**

food coloring

a bowl

a cookie sheet

Look at the cornstarch. Touch it, taste it, smell it. Do the same with the water.

What do you think will happen when you mix the cornstarch and water? What will it look like? Write your answer here.

_____

1. Put the cornstarch in the bowl. Add the water.

2. Stir the mix a bit. Add food coloring if you want.

3. Pour your goo onto a cookie sheet. Watch the way it pours. Poke the goo with your finger.

Is the goo different when you pour it and when you touch it? How?

_____

_____

Was your guess about what would happen right?

_____

Try changing the goo. Add more water. Add more cornstarch. What happens?

_____

_____

It's in the Air

Air is all around us. You can't see air, but you can see things the air pushes. When air moves, we call it **wind**.

Weather Is in the Air

by Keesha

Weather is what is going on in the air around us. The different ways that air, water, and heat mix are what make weather.

Look at this picture. Circle all the things that are being blown by the wind.

You can make a toy helicopter that floats on the air.

1. Take a piece of construction paper. Fold it in half. Then unfold it.

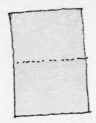

2. On the top half, cut out three triangles like the ones shown.

3. Cut the middle triangle a little more toward the center. Now you have two wings.

4. Fold sides A and B until they meet. Hold them together with a paper clip.

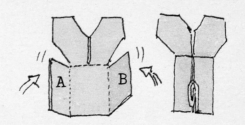

5. Fold one wing forward and one back.

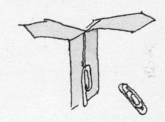

Stand on a stool, and let the helicopter fall. It should spin on the way down. If it doesn't spin, add another paper clip to the bottom.

25

What are we doing up here?

Ms. Frizzle wanted to show us a drizzle.

Water for Clouds
by Arnold

Water on Earth evaporates and rises into the air. That's where the tiny water droplets that make clouds come from.

Clouds are made of very tiny drops of water. Where does the water come from? Heat from the sun makes water on the ground evaporate. You can see how this happens.

1. Take two shallow pans.

2. Measure a quarter cup (about 60 ml) of water into each one.

3. Place one pan in the sun. Place the other in the shade.

4. Come back 3 or 4 hours later. Carefully pour the water from each pan into your measuring cup. Do both pans still have the same amount of water?

5. Try it again. What if you left the water longer? Write what you find in the chart.

MY EVAPORATION CHART

	Where Was the Pan?	How Long?	How Much Water Was Left?
PAN 1			
PAN 2			

The Grass Is Greener

Seeds are one way that plants make new plants. Each plant has its own kind of seed. You can make seeds grow.

1. Fill two plastic cups with dirt.

2. With a pencil, push a small hole into the dirt. Put a seed in each hole, and cover it with dirt.

3. Water your seeds. Make the dirt wet, but not too wet.

4. Place one cup where it will be in the light. Place the second cup in a dark spot, like a closet.

5. Check the cups every few days. Make sure the dirt is just a little wet. Draw what you see in the chart.

What kind of seed did Carlos sow when Carlos sowed a seed?

Did your plants grow? _____

How many days did it take?

_____

Was there any difference between the plant in the light and the plant in the dark?

_____

Day	Plant in the Light	Plant in the Dark
1		
4		
7		
10		

Seed Search

According to my research, a mighty oak can grow from an acorn.

How many different kinds of seeds can you find?

Look in the school yard, on your way home, or at home. See if you can find some of these. Tape or glue them next to their names.

apple seed

sunflower seed

bean seed

rice seed

pine seed (from pinecone)

orange seed

oak seed (acorn)

What other seeds can you find?

Gather your seeds together. Paste them on another sheet of paper. Write the name of each seed. How are the seeds different? How are they the same?

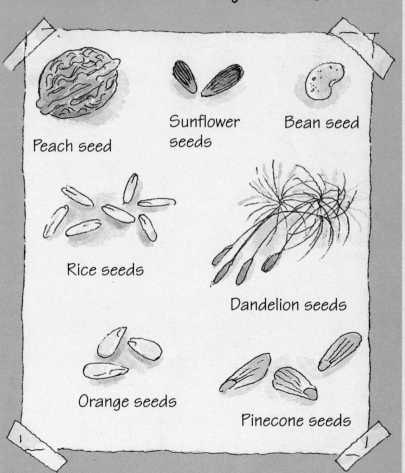

Peach seed

Sunflower seeds

Bean seed

Rice seeds

Dandelion seeds

Orange seeds

Pinecone seeds

Ant Antics

The Queen Ant
by Keesha

In every ant colony there is one queen. She is the only ant that can lay eggs. She is the mother of all the other ants in the nest.

Carlos, what are we doing here?

I thought she said we were going to visit her aunt!

Ants are insects that live and work together. They help each other find food and take care of their young. Each ant has a special job.

An Ant Colony

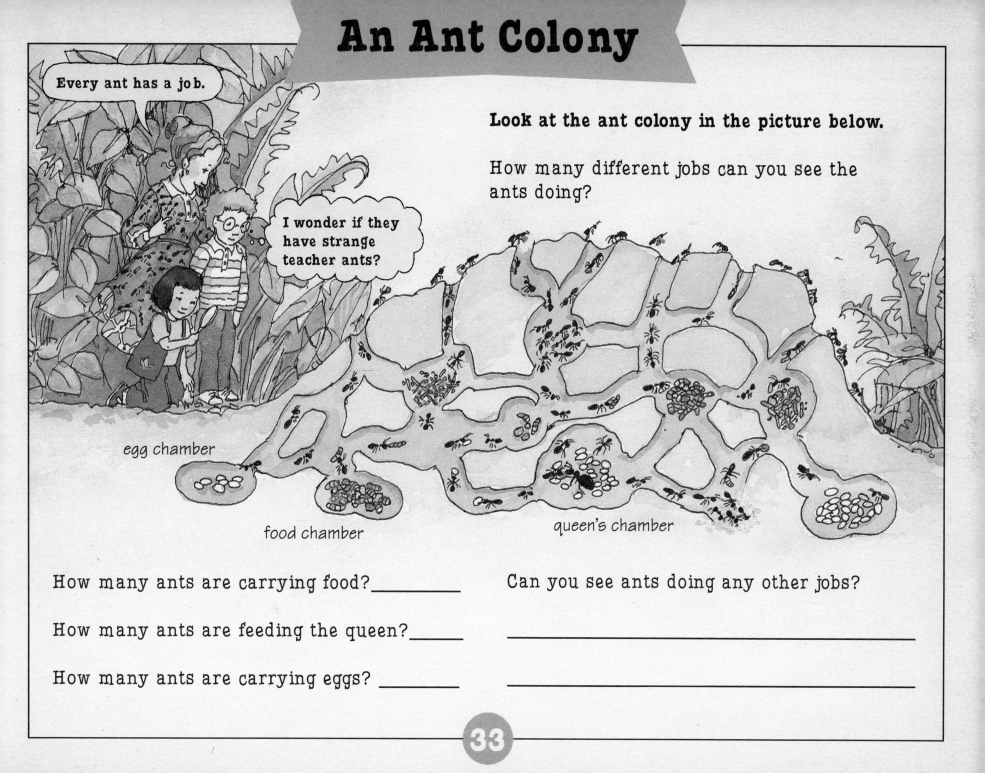

Every ant has a job.

I wonder if they have strange teacher ants?

Look at the ant colony in the picture below.

How many different jobs can you see the ants doing?

egg chamber

food chamber

queen's chamber

How many ants are carrying food?_____

How many ants are feeding the queen?_____

How many ants are carrying eggs? _____

Can you see ants doing any other jobs?

_____

_____

Now Smell This

Ants use smells to send messages.

Why don't they just use the phone?

How Ants Send Messages
by Wanda

Ants use more than smell. They also "talk" to each other by moving their bodies and touching each other.

Ants use their sense of smell a lot.

Ants use smells to tell each other where food is, or if the nest is in danger. Ants from the same nest smell the same. That is one way they tell who belongs in their nest and who doesn't.

Test the noses of your friends. How good is their sense of smell?

Get three things that smell, like peanut butter, an apple, and cheese. Put each one in a small paper bag. Ask some friends to close their eyes and smell each bag.

Use the chart to write down what happens. For each person, make a ✓ if they guess what's in the bag. Make an ✗ if they don't.

How many people guessed what was in all three bags?

_____

Was one smell guessed more than the others?

_____

Name	BAG 1	BAG 2	BAG 3

Home — Not Alone

A Beaver Lodge
by Tim

Beavers dam up rivers to make ponds. Then they build a lodge in the middle of the pond. The entrance to the lodge is underwater.

A Beaver Lodge

I thought Ms. Friz said we were going home.

Yeah, a <u>beaver's</u> home!

Some animals make their homes. Birds make nests. Beavers make lodges.

Other animals find their homes. Bears live in caves. Fish live in lakes and rivers. Deer live in forests. Wherever an animal lives is its home.

Make a model of an animal home.
Learn about one animal and its home.
Draw the animal. Draw its home. Draw
trees or plants that grow close by. Cut out
the pictures and paste them in a shoebox.
Before you start, be sure you know the
answers to these questions.

What animal uses this home?

_____

Did the animal make this home or find it?

_____

What is the home made of?

_____

What does the animal keep in the home?

_____

Home Is Where the Habitat Is

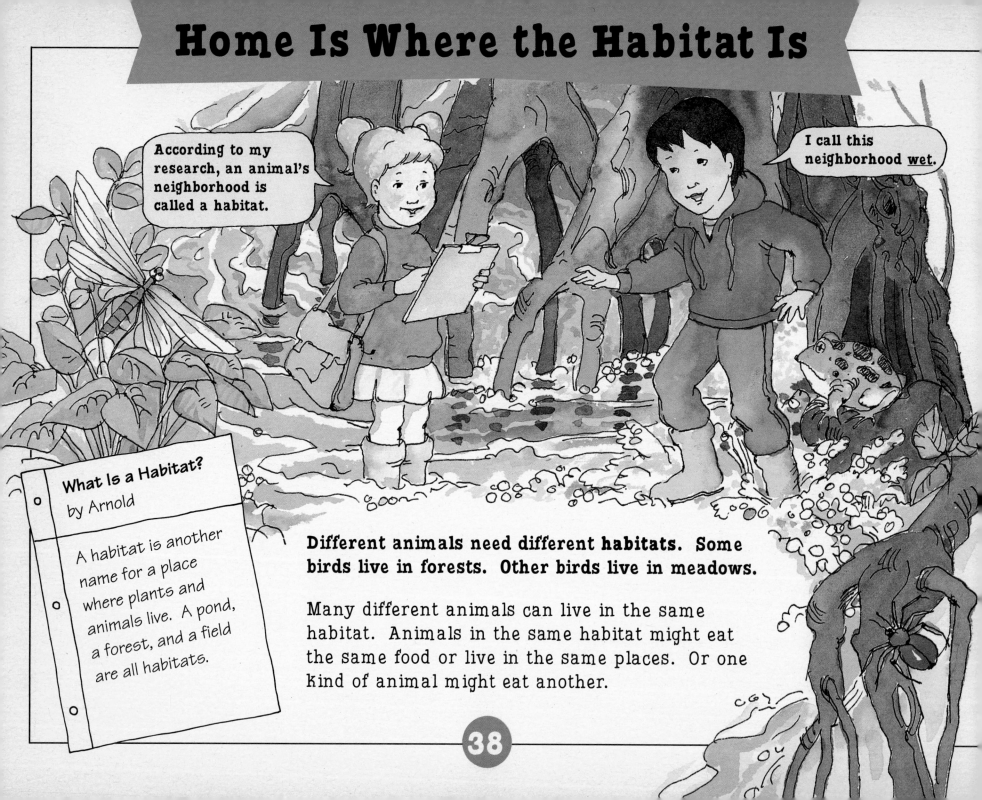

According to my research, an animal's neighborhood is called a habitat.

I call this neighborhood <u>wet</u>.

What Is a Habitat?
by Arnold

A habitat is another name for a place where plants and animals live. A pond, a forest, and a field are all habitats.

Different animals need different habitats. Some birds live in forests. Other birds live in meadows.

Many different animals can live in the same habitat. Animals in the same habitat might eat the same food or live in the same places. Or one kind of animal might eat another.

People live in habitats too.
What is your habitat? Write about it.

What kinds of homes are in your habitat?

_____

What other animals live in your habitat?

_____

Where do the animals get their food?

_____

Draw a picture of your habitat.

MY HABITAT

Zounds!

Class, sound is caused by vibration.

What? We can't hear you! There's too much sound!

Making Music
by Phoebe

Instruments all make sound by vibrating. When you hit a drum, the drum head vibrates. When you strum a guitar, the strings vibrate.

Sounds are made when something shakes, or **vibrates**. When you clap your hands together, you make the air vibrate. That's what makes the noise.

When something shakes the air, it makes sound.

I must be making a lot of sound, because I'm all shook up.

You can make your own instrument.

1. Take a small, dry milk carton. Decorate the outside.

2. Put some small stones, sand, or dried beans inside.

3. Close the carton with tape.

4. Shake the carton to make noise.

Try putting different things in the carton. What kind of sound do small stones make? What about sand? Paper clips? Rubber bands?

Instruments make music by making the air vibrate.

Hold a pot or pan lid by the handle. Tap with a pencil. Does it make a sound?

_____

Now hold the lid. Tap it again. What happened to the sound?

_____

_____

41

Vocal Cords
by Tim

Your vocal cords are in your throat. When you tighten them, you make a high sound. When you loosen them, you make a low sound.

We make sounds with our throats. As the air comes out of our lungs, it makes our **vocal cords** vibrate. Not all animals have vocal cords. Frogs vibrate air in a different way to make frog noises.

See if you can feel the way your throat makes different sounds.

Place your hand on your throat. Make a sound. What does it feel like?

_____

Try making louder sounds, then softer sounds. What happens?

_____

Try talking. What happens now?

_____

Try singing. What happens to your throat when you sing a high note?

_____

A low note?

_____

What's wrong with Arnold?

He's feeling down in the mouth!

43

Ear Parts
by Tim

The outer ear is just one part of your ear. Inside are other parts that help you hear. Never put anything inside your ear—you could hurt your hearing.

We hear with our ears. The part of the ear you can see is called the **outer ear**. The shape of the outer ear helps it collect sound. Other animals have ears that are different shapes.

Would changing the shape of your ear change the way things sound?

Try making different shaped ears. Use paper and tape. You can make ears like an elephant or a rabbit, or ears like a cone or a tube. Put each one up to your own ear, and see what happens. Write down what happens to the sounds you hear. Which shapes help you hear better?

Shape of Ear	What Happened

Something to Chew On

Your Teeth
by Dorothy Ann

You have different kinds of teeth in your mouth. Different teeth do different jobs. Your front teeth are pointy and sharp for biting. Your back teeth are flat for grinding and mashing.

incisors

molars

canines

I think it's time for lunch!

I think we are lunch!

What happens to food when you eat it?

The first place food goes is into your mouth. When you chew your food, you grind it up into little pieces. The watery liquid in your mouth, called **saliva**, helps make the food soft. Now the food is ready for its trip inside your body.

What's inside your mouth?

Pair up with a friend. Have your friend open his or her mouth. Use a flashlight to look inside. Have your friend stick out his or her tongue. Then write about and draw what you see.

1. What different kinds of teeth do you see?

_____

_____

2. What does the tongue look like?

_____

_____

3. Can you see inside the throat? What does it look like?

_____

_____

THIS MOUTH BELONGS TO_____

(your friend's name)

It's a Grind

Your mouth gets food ready to be used by your body.

All this talk about food is making me hungry.

How Your Body Uses Food
by Tim

Your body uses food for energy. It also uses food to build new bones, skin, muscles, and other body parts.

As food travels through your body, it is broken down into smaller and smaller pieces. This is called **digestion**. The first step takes place in your mouth.

1. Take a few raisins. Look at them carefully. Use a magnifying glass if you have one. Draw what you see.

2. Put the raisins in a cup or a bowl. Chop them into little pieces with a knife. Add a little water. Use a fork to mash them. Look at them again. What do they look like now?

3. How is this like what happens when you chew your food?

_____

_____

What Rot!

These mushrooms live on dead wood.

In my old school, we never stood under mushrooms.

What Is Mold?
by Wanda

A mold can be green like a plant, but it is not a plant. Molds live by eating dead plants or animals.

Bread mold

Many plants and animals use dead things for food.

Mushrooms live on dead logs or other dead plants. So do many insects. They break the dead plant into smaller and smaller pieces until it becomes part of the soil.

You can grow mold on a piece of bread.

1. Get two pieces of bread.

2. Sprinkle water on one piece of bread, and put it in a dish. Put it in a dark place.

3. Sprinkle water on another piece of bread. Put it in a dish in the sunlight.

4. Check the bread every day.

When does mold start to show? Does it grow on both pieces? What does the mold look like? Draw what you see.

Where Does Mold Come From?
by Keesha

Mold grows from tiny spores. The spores are in the air all around us. They are so small you can't see them.

	DAY 1	DAY 2	DAY 3	DAY 4	DAY 5	DAY 6
Bread in the Dark						
Bread in the Sun						

Rotten Recycling

Rot is nature's way of recycling.

Worms Recycle
by Arnold

Earthworms are great recyclers. They eat old leaves and other plants. They leave behind soil for new plants to grow in.

When living things die, they begin to rot or decay. They turn into soil and food for other living things. Nature recycles every living thing in this way.

Plan a class recycling center.

What kinds of things will you recycle?
How many bins will you need?

What will go in each bin?
Label the bins in your recycling center.

Is It Catching?

What's a Germ?
by Carlos

A germ is a tiny living thing that gets into your body and makes you sick. Some germs are called bacteria. Some are called viruses.

What is Liz doing?

She wants to catch a cold.

Sometimes germs can make you sick.
You can catch some germs from other people.

Here are some things we can do to help keep from spreading germs:

1. We can cover our mouths when we cough.

2. We can cover our noses with a tissue when we sneeze.

3. We can wash our hands before we eat.

4. We can not share food when we are sick.

5. We can get shots to keep us from getting sick.

6. We can stay home when we have a cold.

Draw a poster to remind people not to spread germs.

Arnold, if you are sick, you can't go on the field trip.

Why didn't I think of this before?

Why Does It Feel Bad to Be Sick?
by Ralphie

When germs get into your body, they make you sick. Your body fights to kill the germs and get rid of them. A fever may help your body fight the germs.

Everyone gets sick sometimes.
What happens when you get sick?
You might have a fever or a sore throat.
You might have a stomachache or a rash.

Just what do you mean by "the pits"?

What does it feel like to be sick?

Find out by talking to people who have been sick. Interview three people. Ask them to name their sickness and describe what it felt like. Then interview yourself.

Look over your interviews. Did everyone feel the same?

Person	Sickness	How he or she felt

Dry Up!

Is a Desert Hot or Cold?
by Tim

A desert can be hot or cold. Some deserts are in very hot places, like the Sahara in Africa. Other deserts are in cold places, like the South Pole.

Sahara Desert

Africa

Ralphie, there isn't much water in the desert.

How about root beer?

A **desert** is a place that is very dry. Many deserts are hot during the day and cold at night. Special plants and animals live in deserts. A cactus is one.

If you were going to a desert, what would you take? Water? A hat? What else?

First, find out what you would find in the desert. Hot sun? Plants with thorns?

Plan a desert survival kit. Write or draw what you would bring.

MY DESERT SURVIVAL KIT

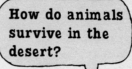

How do animals survive in the desert?

By not lying down on one of those.

What does an animal need to live in the desert?

Different animals have different kinds of bodies. Circle the things you think might help a desert animal.

a thick shell	long legs	swim fins
a fur coat	big ears	a long tail
a fat body	padded feet	a short neck

Now make up your own desert animal. Draw it in the desert above.

Hide from the Heat

Some desert animals hide from the sun.

I'd like to hide from this field trip.

Heat is a problem for many desert animals.

To get out of the heat, they hide from the sun. Some crawl under rocks. Others dig in the sand. Circle the animals hiding in this picture.

**How much cooler is it under the sand?
You can find out.**

1. Fill a deep box with sand. Place it outside in the morning on a hot, sunny day. Then go back in the afternoon.

2. Take a thermometer. Put the end of the thermometer a tiny bit into the sand. After a minute, read the temperature. Write it down in the box marked "Temperature at top of sand."

3. Push another thermometer deep into the sand. Leave it there a minute, then read the temperature. Write it in the box marked "Temperature under sand."

4. Subtract the second number from the first. That's how much cooler it is under the sand.

Temperature at top of sand:

Temperature under sand:

**How much cooler it is
under the sand:**

63

Most of the things you read in this book are true. But some things are made up just for fun. Next to each sentence, write **T** for true or **M** for made up.

— **1.** A school bus can fly into outer space.

— **2.** All living things need food.

— **3.** A lever can help you lift things.

— **4.** You can't see air, but you can see things it pushes.

— **5.** A big oak tree grows from a little acorn.

— **6.** An ant can be taller than Ms. Frizzle.

— **7.** All sounds are caused by vibration.

— **8.** Lizards often wear a hat and boots in the desert.